MW01166145

Super
T
Karate
System

Super T Karate System

With Grand Master Terry "Super T" Gay
Founder Super T Karate System

Super T Karate System

With Grand Master Terry "Super T" Gay
Founder Super T Karate System

Copyright © 2006 by Terry Gay
All Rights Reserved

All rights reserved. No part of this book may be reproduced, stored in a retrieval system, or transmitted in any form or by any means, electronic, mechanical, photocopying, recording, or otherwise, without the prior written permission of Terry Gay.

First Edition
Printed in the United States of America
Published by Super "T" Karate Inc.
ISBN: 1-59824-210-5
Copies of this book may be ordered from

SUPER 'T' KARATE Inc.
4336 Plainfield NE
Grand Rapids, Mich. 49525
(616) 364-5111
www.supertkarate.com

S
U
P
E
R

T

K
A
R
A
T
E

S
Y
S
T
E
M

This is the book that you have been waiting for. It will guide you from White belt to the prestigious Black belt rank.

Dedicated to your progress
Master Terry

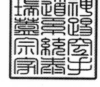

DISCLAIMER

You may be injured if you apply or train in any of the techniques illustrated in this book. Super "T" Karate Inc., Terry Gay and all the parties affiliated with the production and distribution of this book are not responsible for any injuries or illness which may occur by reading and/or doing any of the activities, and/or techniques herein.

This Book is for reference purpose only.

Super "T" Karate Inc. and Terry Gay makes no representation, warranty, or guarantee that the techniques described or illustrated in this book will be safe and effective in a self-defense situation or otherwise.

It is essential that before doing any physical activities you should first consult a physician.

Contents

1 – Acknowledgments

The creation of this book is due to the influence and support over my years in the martial arts with many great people. I'm thanking in print some of the principles and the rest of you know who you are.

My instructors, coaches, students, friends, and family, training and sparring partners. Doyle Gay, Dean Moore, Dan Speaker, Joe Lewis, Jim Kibiloski, Jeff Bradley, Brad Flippen, Jung Lee, Song Lee, Long Bui, Brian Lentz, Bill Chrisman, Mike Bell, William Liqouri, Glen Kemp, Buster Mathis Sr., Kerry Roop, William Burnett, Lloyd Adams, Roy Fisk, Juan Hernandez, Greg Silva, and to my students and SWAT team.

Special thanks to my wife Brenda and my children Nathan, Ryan, TJ, and Leah for the support and understanding for the time and long hours I spent away while working on the Super T Karate System.

Thank you very much for sharing your knowledge and for your support making all of this possible.

Good luck, and best wishes
Grand Master Terry Gay

2 – Foreword

By Mike J

I was approaching 48 years of age and decided that I wanted to make some changes and I thought exercise would be a good place to start. However, I never imagined the difference that Super "T" Karate would make in my life. Training here has more than just improved my level of fitness; it has given me a renewed confidence in myself to achieve physical, mental, spiritual, and emotional goals in my life. The superior guidance that I have received from Terry and the school has been the primary reason I have finally been able to find an exercise that I enjoy and can maintain. Super "T" Karate has a relaxed and welcoming atmosphere, and the people that come here are just great. It is wonderful to walk in and see smiling faces and sweat at the same time and on the same person! There is always someone to talk to, ask questions, and work out with in reality Super "T" Karate has become an escape that refuels me for my everyday life.

Perhaps it would be melodramatic to say that Super "T" Karate changed my life. However, it has started a chain reaction in my life to go after my goals and no longer sit on the sidelines. I plan to keep working toward becoming better at Kickboxing and self-defense. I know that none of this would have come into existence if it had not been for that first phone call to Terry at Super "T" Karate two years ago.

By Anicia L

I have found that Super "T" Karate offers my son both physical skills and essential life skills. The school stresses the importance of respect, focus, and self discipline. It has been an amazing experience to see the students understand the importance of these qualities and use them in other areas of their lives. For my son, positive results have been seen at home and at school.

The results from training here at Super "T" Karate have been more beneficial than any other activity he has had involvement with in the past. His learning process does include working with other students, but ultimately he has a sole responsibility for his achievements. I feel this encourage him to put more of an effort into his training.

The Instructors also add to the whole experience. They provide a positive environment for the students and are extremely patient. They are able to recognize limitation and then challenge the students to exceed them. This is all done with a kind word and encouragement.

By Ann H

Christopher was shy, almost to the point of withdrawn. To even socialize with his classmates took encouragement and sometimes even a scolding. At home, whining seemed to be the norm, rather than the exception. Many times Christopher made statements that he was not good at anything at all.

I never would have considered enrolling any of my children in martial arts. I thought of martial arts as training in violence. When my son came home from school with a pass for a free class at Super T Karate, the last thing I expected was that we would actually be enrolling in the class. However, Christopher showed interest and excitement, so we allowed him to attend the free class.

Since that day, Christopher has developed into a new person. He has developed a respect, not only for his family and friends, but also a respect for himself, acknowledging his talents and self-worth.

Super T Karate has played a priceless role in providing Christopher with incentives and initiatives, and it has taught me as well. Learning martial arts is not learning violent behavior. It is learning principles including respect, confidence, discipline, and honesty, and Super T Karate has certainly excelled in their teaching.

Christopher continues to grow in confidence and respect. I love the enthusiasm he shows, striving to better himself every class. I love the look of pride in him with each new accomplishment. Each day I see him setting new goals, whether big or small, and Super T Karate has played a vital role in his mission to accomplish them.

Thank you Super T Karate!!!!

By Russ and April

When our children first enrolled at Super T Karate they were facing a move into a new school system. Both of them, typically shy individuals, were forced to move out of their comfort zone, not an easy task for anyone and especially difficult for my 8 year old. Within weeks of enrollment Master Terry and his staff had both of the boys performing at a physical level that could never be challenged by typical youth sports, and we tried them all! More importantly, because of the results that the boys themselves noticed, their self-esteem immediately improved. We watched as each week passed by the perpetual development and enhancement of their focus, self-discipline, and determination levels. The values that the staff helps to instill into the students reach far into their personal and adult lives. The constant positive reinforcement that all the students receive from the staff has turned our two "shy" boys into young adults who cannot wait for their next opportunity to perform with their Demo Team.

Super T Karate Rocks!!

By Tim & Tricia

We are finally getting the opportunity to know our son after eight-years of uncertainty. With ADHD building a barrier around him, it is as if his true identity has been hidden. Dylan has struggled to find something that would break down these barriers and let him show his family, and the world, which he really is. After attempting to find assistance from a variety of resources, we finally found help at Super T Karate. The instructors and staff of Super T Karate provide the encouragement that Dylan needed to gain confidence in his ability to be successful. Because he has learned the rewards of mutual respect, Dylan has positively changed his attitude toward himself and others. His hard work, dedication, and determination to improve himself are all a result of the personal involvement the people of Super T Karate show in each individual child.

Thank-you Team Super T Karate!

3 – Biography of Grand Master Terry Gay

Master Terry was born on May 23, 1960 to Jean and Doyle Gay. His first introduction to the martial arts was by his father who showed him some of the hand-to-hand combat techniques that he learned while serving in the military during World War II.

In 1972 at the age of twelve, Terry started his formal education in the martial arts by taking classes in Tang Soo Do Moo Duk Kwan. He has been an active practitioner of the martial arts ever since. Terry currently holds the rank of 9th degree black belt & 6th degree black belt certified by Black Belt Hall of Fame member and karate/kickboxing legend Joe Lewis. The Super T Karate System is recognized by the (ISHH) International Society of Headfamilies & Headfounders, United States Martial Arts Association (USMAA), UMAHoF Supreme Sokeship Council, International Soke~Head Founder Society (ISHFS), and the World Union of Sokes.

Over the years Terry has earned, and still holds, black belt ranking in the martial arts styles of Tae Kwon Do, Tang Soo Do Moo Duk Kwan, and American Karate. He has also gained "real world" experience by working as a bouncer and security guard as well as being a professional boxer and kickboxer. On September 5, 1998, the World Head of Family Sokeship Council in Orlando, Florida inducted Master Terry into the International Martial Arts Hall of Fame as Master Instructor of the Year. On June 26, 2004 the World Karate union Hall of Fame awarded Master Terry for his time and achievements in the Martial Art with the Golden Life Time Achievement award. July 24, that same year Super T Karate was inducted into the Universal Martial Arts Hall of Fame as Outstanding Kickboxing School of the Year.

February 1, 1986, Terry won the P.A.K.A. (Professional American Karate Association) World Middleweight title by knocking out Kit Lykins in the 3rd round of a scheduled 12 round fight, in Battle

Creek, Michigan. With a fighting career that spanned more than 30 professional boxing and kickboxing bouts, he gained world contender ship as the P.A.K.A. #1 middleweight contender, KICK #3 world cruiserweight contender, and the #2 P.A.K.A. light heavyweight contender. Many of Terry's fights have been televised on national and local cable channels and ESPN and PASS cable networks.

Certified Black Belt Ranks
* 9th Degree Youshiki Soke (ISHH) Super T Karate / Kickboxing System
* 6th Degree Black Belt Certified by Joe Lewis Karate Systems
* 4th Degree Black Belt Tae Kwon Do
* 4th Degree Black Belt Tang Soo Do Moo Duk Kwan

Professional Fighting
* World PAKA Middleweight Kickboxing Champion (PAKA)
* #1 World Middleweight Contender (PAKA)
* #3 World Cruiserweight Contender (KICK)
* #5 World Light Heavyweight Contender (PAKA)
* Professional Boxer

**World P.A.K.A title fight in Battle Creek
Michigan 1986.**

**Master Terry KO'ing Kit Lykins
winning the world P.A.K.A. title.**

On Guard.

**Testing for his 6ᵗʰ Degree with 10ᵗʰ Degree
Grand Master Joe Lewis.**

Testing for his 6th Degree with 10th Degree Grand Master Joe Lewis.

Nathan and Ryan Gay.

Nathan's Side Kick.

**Winning the world P.A.K.A middleweight kickboxing
title belt from Kit Lykins.**

Master Terry with his world title belt.

Receiving his 6th degree black belt in the Joe Lewis Karate/Kickboxing System.

Ryan Gay.

**Master Terry and Joe Lewis after a
sparring session.**

Lets get ready to rumble.

Nathan Gay one of the designated inheritors of the Super T System.

Master Terry's favorite kick.

**Ryan Gay one of the designated
inheritors of the Super T System.**

Samurai Terry

Master Terry and Don (the dragon) Wilson.

**Master Terry with 5x world
kickboxing champion Kathy Long.**

**Master Terry and Mike working on
Knife fighting.**

Master Terry with two of his sons.

**Master Terry working on
punch defense.**

Nathan and Ryan sparring.

**Master Terry working on
Kickboxing set #3.**

Nathan (Samurai Kid) Gay.

Take that big brother.

Nathan and Ryan Sparring.

Master Terry left hook.

Leah

Super T Family

4 – Credit & Awards

Association Memberships & Certifications
* (ISHH) International Society of Headfamilies & Headfounders
* United States Martial Arts Association (USMAA)
* World Union of Sokes (WUS)
* UMAHoF Supreme Sokeship Council
* International Soke~Head Founder Society (ISHFS)
* Cobra Martial Arts Association (CMAA)
* Member Black Belt Schools International (BBSI)
* Joe Lewis Black Belt Association (JLBBA)
* K.I.K.A. / K.B.M.A. Grand Masters Council
* International Sung Ja Do Association (ISA)
* Would Martial Arts Organizations Alliance Master Council (WMAOA)

* International Combat Martial Arts Unions Association (ICMAUA)
* Certified by the International Mixed Martial Arts Association (IMMA)

Association Positions
* State Director International Society of Headfamilies & Headfounders
* WMAOA Master Council
* President Super T Karate Association

Instructor Certifications
* Certified Defense Tactic Instructor --- Controlled F.O.R.C.E
* Black Belt Schools of America Certified Instructor
* Certified Ground Force Instructor
* Certified SHOOTFIGHTING Instructor
* United States Martial Arts Association
* Founder S.R.C. Street Reality Combat System
* CMAA International Instructor Certification
* Master Instructor (ISA)

Media – Newspaper - Seminars
* Featured in Video segment for the United Professionals
* Boxed on PASS TV
* Kickboxed on ESPN
* Featured in Orlando Sentinel Newspaper
* Interviewed on Channel 8 News
* Producer and Instructor of Combat Kickboxing DVD / Video Tape Series
* Author Combat Kickboxing Book
* Interviewed by Fox TV News
* Seminar presenter for United Professional
* Grand Valley TV

Awards and Recognition
* Master Instructor World Sokeship Council Martial Arts Hall of Fame

* IMMA Hall of Fame
* Ruby Award United Professionals
* Five Star Service Black Belt School of America
* Golden Life Time Achievement World Karate Union Hall of fame
* Grand Master Kickboxing Instructor of the year UMAHoF
* Bravery Award Branch County Sheriff Dept

Training Instructors and Mentors
* Joe Lewis – Full Contact Karate / Kickboxing
* Mike Bell -- Kickboxing
* William Liqouri-- Kickboxing
* Dean Moore – Tang Soo Do Moo Duk Kwan / TKD
* Dan Speaker – Tang Soo Do Moo Duk Kwan
* Greg Silva – Martial Arts Business
* Glen Kemp -- Boxing
* Buster Mathis Sr. -- Boxing
* Song Lee – Tae Kwon Do
* Juan Hernandez – Martial Arts Business
* Brian Lentz – Kickboxing

5 – Super T Karate System

The Super 'T' Karate System was founded in 1983 on the 12th day of November by Terry Gay as a personal quest for a practical self-defense system for the real world. This system is designed to produce effective results in realistic situations, keeping in mind that real conflicts bear no resemblance to what occurs in the comfort of a training facility. This system will have no limitations, because we will always be adding and upgrading the techniques and practical concepts.

The techniques of the Super 'T' Karate System are based on the natural movements and actions of the body rather than a prearranged pattern of moves. The Super 'T' Karate students train using dynamic concepts, scientific approaches, realistic applications, and just plain common sense so they can and will act on instinct, rather than on memory, when responding to an attack in today's real world.

The Super "T" System effectiveness has been proven on more than one occasion on the professional fighting level and in real life self defense. This explosive and effective system can be integrated into any style or system of the martial arts.

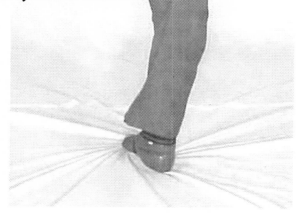

BENEFITS OF THE SUPER 'T' SYSTEM

- Self Defense for the Real World

- Improve Flexibility

- Increase Agility

- Increase Awareness

- Increase Endurance

- Improve Coordination

- Accuracy

- Increase Power

- Increase Speed

- Stress Release

- Improved Self Esteem

- Improved Self Discipline

- Improved Confidence

- Improved Health

PHILOSOPHY

** Never change what works.

** Learn whatever you can, and never close your mind to something different. Always keep an open mind.

** Know yourself.

** Never limit yourself.

** To be in 100 percent physical shape, you must first be in 100 percent mental shape.

** Always respect your judgment, as you can't fool yourself. Go with your instinct.

** Take defeat as a learning process.

** Never think negatively, always be positive.

** Progress with the times.

** Beat the pain, as pain is your enemy.

** Be the best that you can be.

** Train for real – To be prepared.

6 – Student Creed

STUDENT CREED

I will develop myself in a positive manner, and avoid anything that could reduce my mental growth and physical health.

I will develop self-discipline in order to bring out the best in myself and others.

I will use common sense before self-defense.

This is a Black Belt School – I'm Dedicated - I'm Motivated I'm on a Quest to be my Best. **Ashhh**

7 – Stretching

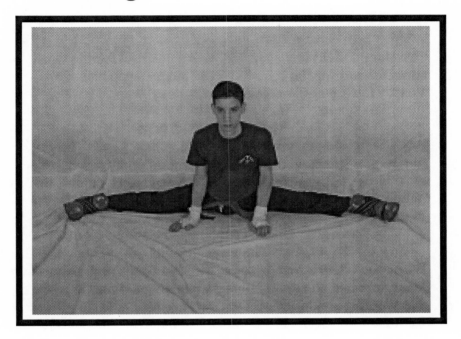

What is flexibility? Flexibility is the elasticity of a muscle. Anyone, no matter what size or age can improve his or her flexibility.

What is stretching? Stretching is what you do to get a muscle or muscle group ready for activities. Be aware that there is a difference between flexibility and stretching, although you must do stretching to increase your flexibility. Whenever you are stretching, take it slow, especially in the beginning. Let your mind and body adjust to the stress of the activity.

You should stretch lightly before any type of workout and make sure that you stretch the muscle groups you will be using within your workouts. It is my opinion through many years of training in the martial arts that you should never stretch for flexibility before a workout. Do your flexibility stretching after your workout so your muscles are all warmed up, this will help reduce injuries. Remember that you should warm the muscle up before you do any type of stretching.

Stretching should feel good and have a peaceful feeling when done correctly on a regular basis. You can stretch everyday. **WARNING**: you should never over stretch.

HOW TO STRETCH

Before you stretch you must first warm up your muscles. You can do this by doing push ups, jumping jacks, or running in place. After you break a sweat you can start into your stretching.

The Easy Stretch

When you begin a stretch, spend 10-30 seconds in the easy stretch. Make sure that you don't bounce when you do this. Go to the point that you feel a mild tension, and relax as you hold the stretch. The feeling of the tension as you hold the stretch should subside as you hold that position. If it does not, ease off slightly and find a degree of tension that is comfortable. The easy stretch helps to loosen up the muscle for the developmental stretch.

The Developmental Stretch

After the easy stretch, move a fraction of an inch further until you again feel tension and hold for 10-30 seconds. Again the tension should diminish; if not, ease off slightly.

Breathing

Your breathing should be slow, and under control. If you are bending forward to do a stretch, exhale as you bend forward and then breath slowly as you hold the stretch.

Do not hold your breath while stretching.

Side Lunge

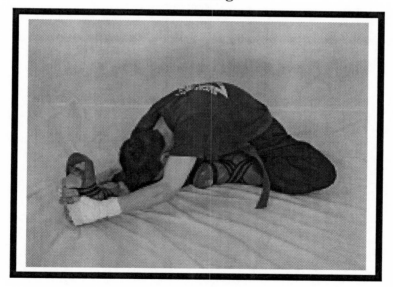

In Leg

Straddle

Head to knee in Straddle stretch

Palms to Floor

American Splits

Side Splits

8 – Hand Wrapping

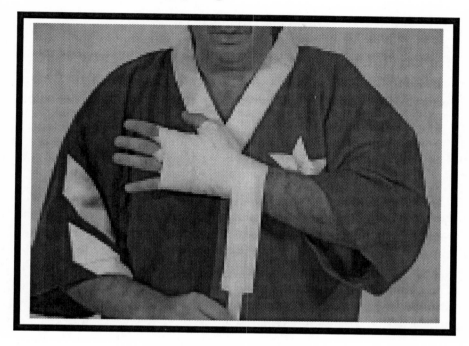

HAND WRAPPING

It is highly recommended that you wrap your hands prior to any kind of equipment training or sparring. The wraps help by making your hands and wrist less susceptible to strains, bruising, and other types of injuries. I personally never spar or do any type of bag work without my hands wrapped.

HAND WRAPPING POINTERS

The object when wrapping your hands is to protect the bones and joints. Here are a couple of key points to remember when you are wrapping your hands. **1)** Keep tension on the wraps as you wrap around your hands. **2)** Do the wrapping in a way that it pulls the joints back towards your wrist. Do this by going through your fingers and around the thumb with the wraps. **3)** As you wrap your hand make sure that you kris cross the wrap on the back of the hand; this will help your hand from bucking down.

Be careful not to wrap your hands so tightly that it cuts off the circulation in your hands. After you finish wrapping your hands you can apply some tape over the wrap to help secure the wrap.

HOW TO WRAP YOUR HANDS

(1) Put the thumb through the thumb loop and wrap twice around your wrist **(2)** Take the wrap and go between the pinkie finger, wrapping it under the hand and bringing the wrap back up and around the thumb base. **(3)** Continue going between the middle fingers and wrapping under the hand, coming back up and around the thumb base. **(4)** Next wrap between your index finger and middle finger, taking the wrap around the index finger and go back towards the wrist. **(5)** Go half way around the wrist and up and over the thumb taking the wrap around the thumb and back towards the wrist. **(6)** Go half way around the wrist coming up and over the top of the hand and wrap around the thumb one more time. **(7)** Then go back towards the wrist, around the wrist and over the back of the hand. **(8)** Wrap over the knuckles two times then go back and use the remainder of the wrap around the wrist and secure the end of the wrap.

Make a fist to check that the wrap is tight but not overly tight. If the wrap feels good then you can wrap some tape around and over the hand wrap to secure and tighten it even more.

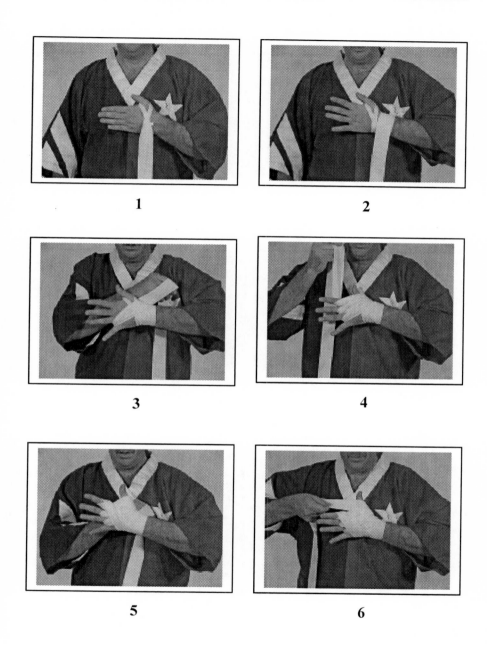

1

2

3

4

5

6

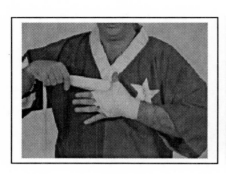

7

8

9

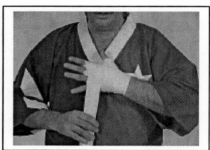

10

11

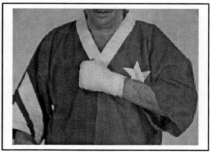

Finished

9 – Footwork

FOOTWORK

The effectiveness of your punching, kicking, and grappling techniques depends on your footwork. In order to use your hands and feet effectively, your feet must first be put in the correct position to attack.

If you are slow on your feet your punches and kicks will also be slow.

The better your footwork is, the easier it will be to avoid punches, kicks, and takedowns. You should never fire your technique until your opponent is within range. Keep on the balls of your feet with a slight bounce up and down and your knees slightly bent.

MOVEMENT

Your movement should be as fluid as possible. You want to glide around by sliding on the bottom of your feet lightly along the ground. If you are a right-handed fighter and you want to move backward or to the right, move you back foot first. If you want to move forward or to the left, your front foot should move first. If you are left-handed, the opposite would apply.

When ever you move your front foot, slide the back foot along. You should never stand or move flat-footed. You can keep your back heel slightly off the ground so you may pivot and react faster at any given time.

Remember to always keep your body loose and limber, never strong or tight. This way you will be able to move and react much faster. If you are tight, you will move much slower and use a lot more energy.

MOBILITY

In order to punch or kick effectively you must accurately judge the distance to your opponent. This reduces their ability to move out of the way. Remember your attack will not succeed unless you are at the correct distance the moment you fire your technique.

SAFE ZONE

A safe zone is when you and your opponent have to step forward in order to attack. Use constant movement when you are in your safe zone so your opponent will have a hard time judging your distance. This way you can make your opponent misjudge their distance on you while you keep the correct distance for yourself. Whenever attacking from a distance it is wise to use the longest weapon, closest to your target.

10 – Stance

FIGHTING STANCE

Your fighting stance is the foundation of all of your techniques. The fighting stance gives you strong balance with evasive footwork capabilities. Some styles and systems have many different stances. The Super "T" Karate system has just one major stance the guard/fighting stance.

This stance offers great protection, mobility, balance, and leverage so you can execute fast strong techniques. This one stance is highly effective in all three ranges of fighting.

SETTING INTO YOUR STANCE

If you are right handed place your left foot forward and your right foot in back. If you are left-handed your right foot will be forward with your left foot in back. Always place your power hand the furthest from your opponent.

How to set into your stance:

(1) Stand with your feet about shoulder width apart. **(2)** Raise your fist up to the level of your chin and tuck your elbows close to your body with your chin tucked down towards your chest. **(3)** Move your power side foot back, so your feet are about 1 to 1 1/2 shoulder widths apart, with the back foot pointing to the side. Point your front foot forward. **(4)** Then move your back foot over about 3-4 inches while bending at both knees slightly, distributing your body weight equally over both feet. **(5)** You can also raise the heel of your back foot slightly off the ground. **(6)** Make sure that your body is facing your target sideways, pointing your front foot at your opponent.

This will help make your stance more mobile and allow for faster movement. If you are right handed and fighting a left hander make sure that you keep your front foot on the outside of their front foot, this keeps you away from their power side while simultaneously giving you a better angle of attack. Doing this will give you better balance with more power in your punches.

11 – Defense

BLOCKING TECHNIQUES

In the Super "T" Karate System you will find several different types of blocks. Blocks are normally for defense, but they can also be used as strikes or to set up counter strikes.

Don't limit yourself to the blocks found only in this section. You can use any part of your body to effectively evade, block, or stop any type of technique.

Most of the blocks found in the Super "T" Karate System are done with the front hand, leaving your power hand free to counter strike. These blocks can also be done with the backhand. Remember to return your hand back to position after a block is completed.

LOW BLOCK

The low block is used to guard the mid and lower section of the body. It is usually thrown with the front hand because it is closest to your opponent. But as with all of the blocks it also can be done with the backhand.

When executing the low block from the fighting stance, move the arm at the elbow and shoot straight down with your hand going about 3-4 inches past your leg. Remember to chamber the hand after the execution.

When using the low block against a front kick don't meet the kick straight on. You will want to make the impact on the side of the leg, not the top of the shin. This way you deflect the kick instead of meeting power with power.

HIGH BLOCK

In the fighting stance, the high block is used against straight techniques to the face and techniques coming down on top of the head. Again your front hand will be the main blocking arm.

To execute the high block, raise the arm with the elbow and forearm going above the head on a 45-degree angle, with your palm facing outward and the bottom part of your fist facing upwards.

INWARD BLOCK

The inward block, also referred to as the middle block, is usually done with the front hand. The inward block is used to protect the head, ribs, neck, and solar plexus.

When executing the inward block with your front hand, twist your front foot just like you do when you throw a front hand hook punch. Keep the forearm straight up and down, and then push the arm out and past your body towards the inside.

OUTWARD BLOCK

Executing the outward block from your fighting stance is a simple movement of just thrusting the elbow, forearm and hand at the same time to the outside of your body to guard against techniques that are coming from your blind side.

CHECK BLOCK

The check block is actually a parry that is used to deflect straight punches coming at your head or face. The check block can be performed with the front or backhand depending on which punch you are blocking.

When executing the check block, open up the hand so you will strike with the palm. Remember not to reach out while doing this block because it leaves you wide open for counters. You should do this block close to your body, so your opponent's strike is at its extension.

When executing a check block, tilt your head in the opposite direction of the block. This will get your head out of your opponent's line of fire.

60

V-BLOCK

The V-block is a highly effective block to use against the haymaker, roundhouse, and looping types of punches going to the head.

To execute the V-block from the fighting stance with your front hand, keep your arm tight and raise your elbow so it comes up level with your forehead, with the hand going back to protect the back of your head.

When executing the V-block with your backhand, apply the same technique as with the front hand. The only difference is that you turn your back foot forward towards your opponent.

DEFENSE

Defensive skills may be the most difficult for the student to master because it is much easier to be on the offensive. With your offensive skills you are initiating the action and you know what you are going to do next. When you are on the defensive you are reacting to your opponent's actions and movements. Becoming a good defensive fighter takes good reactions, quick thinking, and good instincts along with practicing a lot of training drills.

The first step in having a good defense has more to do with a good offense. You must never fight relying solely on your defensive skills.

The key to any good defense is to keep your opponent concerned about your offensive skills. When working on your defensive skills it is good to work with someone at a lower level. This allows you to acquire your defensive skills without having to use such a strong offense.

Footwork, blocking, ducking, slipping, trapping, and strong offensive skills are a must for your defense.

GUARDS AND BLOCKING

A good guard is made by keeping the hands in close to your face and keeping the elbows held tight to your body. The upper torso should be turned sideways, with the lead shoulder pointing at your opponent, to protect your midsection. When you are in this position, your opponent will have a difficult time penetrating your defense. You should be able to block 90% of the blows to your body by taking them on your arms.

SLIPPING DRILL

Square off with your partner in your fighting stance. Designate one person to throw the jabs first. When throwing your jabs make sure to your throw them straight at the forehead. Take your time, start out slow, and remember this is a learning drill. When the jab comes at you, move your head slightly to one side or the other making the jab miss you. The more you practice this drill the faster your partner will be able to throw the jabs. Remember to start slow and don't double up on the jabs.

BOB & WEAVE DRILL

Both you and your partner get into a fighting stance close to each other. One person will start with a right hook punch to the body then a right hook to the head. As the hook to the head comes at you, break at the waist and bend your knees slightly ducking towards the punch and under it, keeping as close to your partner as possible and coming up on the other side of the punch. Then your partner will throw a left body hook followed with a left head hook. Repeat the bob & weave in the opposite direction. This will complete your turn. Now return the punches to your partner. Remember start out slow.

COUNTER ATTACKS

In order to counter you must first avoid your opponent's attack. This leaves you in a good position to throw a counter strike by giving you an exposed target. You can feint or use a fake to set up your counter strike by making your opponent react to your movements. Counter striking is not a defensive action but a valuable method of fighting

TAKEDOWN DEFENSE

The most feared tactic for any stand up fighter is to be taken down to the ground. We as stand up fighters can utilize strategies to prevent us from being taken to the ground. Just like any of the exercises and techniques, we must practice them in order for them to have any effect in a real combat situation. If these moves are utilized and practiced to their fullest extent they will give you an advantage.

SPRAWL

The sprawl is a wrestling technique that is used when your opponent shoots in for a tackle, single or double leg takedown. He will have their head even to or below your waist.

As your opponent shoots in push his head down and shoot your legs back out of reach. If your opponent has one of your legs, shoot the other back away as far as you can and drop all of your weight on his back taking him to the ground, face and chest first. Immediately move to his back so you can finish him.

12 – Punches

PUNCHING TECHNIQUES

The punches found in the Super "T" Karate system are the same ones that are found in Western boxing. Your hands are the Super T Karate System primary weapons, simply because they are used for almost everything that we as humans do, thus making the movements more coordinated and natural.

The Super "T" student uses four basic punches: the jab, power, hook, and uppercut. The jab and power punches are used more in the mid - range, while the hook and uppercuts are used more in the inclose range. The hook and uppercut can be performed with both the front and backhands.

The Super "T" Karate student utilizes two other punching techniques - the back fist and ridge hand.

PUNCHING POINTERS

To deliver effective punches the following must be applied to their execution.

1. Execute each punch directly from the fighting stance - without winding up - to avoid giving the punch away.

2. Keep your hands up in the chambering position and bring your hands back just as fast as they go out after completing a punch.

3. Keep your shoulders and arms loose when punching - only tighten the body and arm after you make contact.

4. Bring your punching shoulder up to protect your chin, at the same time keeping the opposite hand up protecting the chin.

5. Concentrate on putting your body behind each punch for maximum power. Keep your knees bent and twist your feet the same direction as you throw the punch.

TARGETS FOR YOUR PUNCHES

** **Nose**
** **Chin**
** **Eye Socket**
** **Temple**
** **Cheek**
** **Throat**
** **Shoulder**
** **Chest**
** **Solar Plexus**
** **Groin**
** **Neck**
** **Liver**

JAB PUNCH

Your jab hand, also referred to as the "range finder", is the one that is the closest to your opponent. The main purpose of the jab is to keep your opponent off balance and at bay. It is also used as a sight for your combinations. If you can't hit them with your jab punch then they are out of range for any other punches. The jab is the beginning point of a combination. Your jab punch is a mid-range strike.

To throw a successful jab you must have good judgment of timing and distance. Targets for the jab are the nose, chin, eye, throat, shoulder, temple, chest, solar plexus, and groin.

When you throw your jab make sure that you throw it as straight as possible and keep your elbows close to your body. This makes it much harder to detect.

DOUBLE JAB

The double jab is a very effective technique to close the distance between you and your opponent. Throw a jab out and, as you bring it back, shuffle forward and fire a second jab.

If the first jab misses, the second one will probably hit its target. It's very hard to defend against a good double jab.

THROWING THE JAB PUNCH

When you fire your jab out, your punching arm should go out in a straight path towards your target. Keep your elbow below the hand with the shoulder rolled up to protect the chin. At the same time keep your chin tucked down. On impact your hand and shoulder should be at the same level. Your palm should be facing the floor when the punch is fully extended.

To give more impact to the punch slide your front foot forward as you make contact. Remember to chamber your hand back and bring your foot back after the completion of the jab punch.

JAB PUNCHING POINTERS

1) At the same time you fire the jab out pivot at your hips thrusting your shoulder into the punch.

2) Slide your front foot forward for more power, but don't forget to bring it back.

3) Keep your power hand up to guard your face.

4) Bring the hand back faster than it goes out.

5) Your jab shoulder should rotate up to protect your chin against any possible counters to the face.

6) Jab straight off your shoulder - never punch down.

7) Twist your palm down at the extension of the punch.

8) To jab at the body, bend your knees to get to the same height as the target you are attacking.

9) Use the jab to the body to lower your opponent's hands, opening their head to attack.

10) Keep your elbows in.

11) Snap out the punch like you would a towel

POWER PUNCH

The power punch is usually the second punch in a combination. It is also used as an effective counter punch to the jab or a kick. When you throw this punch remember to bring your shoulder up and twist your palm down. The power punch is a mid-range strike.

Targets for this knockout punch are the nose, chin, eye, temple, ear, cheek, throat, shoulder, chest, groin, solar plexus, and neck.

When you fire this punch make sure that you throw the punch straight out and keep your elbows in close to your body. Bring the punching shoulder up to protect your chin from counters. Bend at your knees, twist the back foot so the toes point straight at the target and at the same time go up on the ball of the back foot. Make sure that you keep your feet planted.

Most of all make sure that you are in range and not reaching or lunging for your opponent.

THROWING THE POWER PUNCH

When throwing this knockout punch, just like your jab, throw your punch in a straight line to your target. Keep your elbow below the hands with the shoulder rolling up to protect the chin. At the same time keep your chin tucked down.

Twist the back foot the same direction as the punch. At the extension of the power punch you should be up on the ball of the back foot with your knees slightly bent and your hips and shoulders twisted slightly for maximum power and distance. Your palm should be facing the floor. You can slide your back foot towards the target increasing the power. Just like the jab, the hand should come back to the chin after the punch is thrown.

POWER PUNCHING POINTS

1) Twist your feet the same direction as your punch.

2) Shift your body weight forward to the front foot as you deliver the punch.

3) Stiffen your arm as soon as you make contact.

4) Keep your other hand up to protect your chin.

5) Bend your knees.

6) Twist your hips and shoulders into the punch.

7) You can slide you back foot forward as you make contact to increase the power.

8) Keep your elbows in.

9) Punch straight out.

HOOK PUNCHES

Hook punches are a close quarters punch that can be executed while almost standing on top of your opponent. The hook punch, when thrown correctly is probably one of the most devastating punches in this system. While throwing the hook punch keep your elbows in close to your body.

Hook punches can be used effectively for counter punching - it is a very difficult punch to defend against.

Hook punches are easy to integrate into your combination because they flow with almost any type of technique. The nose, check, eye, temple, groin, neck, throat, shoulder, liver, and solar plexus all make great targets for this punch.

THROWING THE HOOK PUNCH

To throw the devastating front hand hook punch, lift your elbow away from the body and start twisting your front foot and body the same direction that you are punching, keeping the elbow below the punching hand. As you make impact pull your hand back towards your back shoulder to increase the power in the punch. Keep your elbow and hand at the same level. While looking straight ahead your punching shoulder should come up and protect the chin. The other hand should also be up protecting the chin.

Your backhand hook is thrown basically the same way except you twist on the back foot.

HOOK PUNCHING POINTERS

1) Keep your feet planted.

2) Shift your weight to the back leg when you throw the punch.

3) Keep the other hand up to protect the chin.

4) Twist the feet the same direction as the punch.

5) Keep your punching elbow lower than the punching hand when you fire the hook punch.

6) As you twist go up on the ball of your front foot when executing a front hand hook punch, and twist on the ball of the back foot when executing a backhand hook punch.

7) Twist the back foot when throwing the backhand hook.

8) Keep your elbows in close to your body.

UPPERCUT PUNCHES

The uppercut, like the hook punch, is also a close quarters punch. The targets for this punch are the nose, chin, chest, groin, and liver. This is a highly effective punch to throw when you are fighting on the inside. One of the best times to throw the uppercut punch is when you see the back of your opponent's head.

When throwing the backhand uppercut bend at your knees and twist your back foot. As you go up on the ball of the foot, twist it the same direction that you are punching. At the same time bring the hand and arm up on a short arc straight up with your elbow down. Your hand should never go higher than your head.

The front hand uppercut is thrown almost the same way with a minor adjustment. Your front foot will twist and the toes will go the same direction as your groin and not at your target.

THROWING THE UPPERCUT PUNCH

When throwing the backhand uppercut you need to bend slightly to the punching side so you get the hand below its target. Keep your elbow in close to the body then shoot the hand straight up in a short arc, while at the same time twisting your back foot straight ahead going up on the ball of your back foot.

Throwing the front hand uppercut is done almost the same way as the backhand except that your front foot will twist to point to the side of your body, with the back foot going the same way.

UPPERCUT PUNCHING POINTS

1) Don't advertise your punch by winding up.

2) Tilt your body over the hip on the same side you are punching.

3) Never let your hand go above your head when your throw this punch.

4) Keep your elbows in.

BACKFIST

The back fist, like the jab, is executed with the front hand. The striking surfaces are the knuckles and back of the hand. Main targets for the back fist are the nose, eye, check, temple, and groin. The back fist is a very effective weapon to use against an opponent that is good at slipping because of its sweeping motion. Your back fist when thrown effectively will actually follow the head movement of a slip.

When executing the back fist, throw it from the elbow in a wiping motion that is really a snap and is very difficult to slip.

BACKFIST POINTERS

1) Don't have too much tension in the arm, as this will slow the strike down - keep your arm loose as you execute the back fist.

2) Do not over extend your arm or elbow this can injure the joints.

3) Bring the hand back faster than it goes out.

13 – Kicks

KICKING TECHNIQUES

The kicks used by the Super 'T' Karate student are not of the flashy type. These kicks can and are used for real self-defense. The Super "T" student utilizes four basic kicks: the front kick, side kick, round kick, and hook kick. These kicks are used to keep your opponent at bay and can be done standing, moving, jumping, or spinning. Remember that in a real self-defense situation you probably will be wearing some type of shoes giving you a much harder striking surface.

Although the legs are stronger than the arms they only account for about 25% of all knockouts in competition. This is because kicks are less accurate and are easier to avoid. Knowing this, it is most important to follow your punching techniques with your kicks to make the kicks harder to see and defend against.

Kicks can be a great asset. With skill in kicking you can injure your opponent or keep them at a safe distance. Remember that there is a real difference between sport and real self-defense kicks.

KICKING EXECUTION

More important than the actual extension of the leg is the positioning of the knee and foot - this is referred to as the chamber. This is done by bringing the kicking leg knee up as high as your target just prior to kicking. The initial position/chamber movement will give you greater thrusting power, speed, and mobility. When the knee is high your supporting leg knee should be slightly bent for balance, with your hands up protecting the face. When sparring or fighting keep your kicks down low to bring down your opponents guard, allowing you to go up high with your hand strikes.

KICKING POINTS

1) Raise the knee up just as high as your target.

2) Keep the knee and foot between you and your target.

3) When kicking, raise the knee up just like you are going to use it for a knee strike. This will keep you from kicking from the floor, making the kick faster and more accurate.

4) Kick with your leg first and body second.

5) After throwing your kick return it to the floor as fast as it goes out.

6) Try not to telegraph your kick.

REMEMBER THIS

Your kicks are for outside or long range fighting, as they are used to keep your opponent on the outside and away from you.

You can also use them for setting up other techniques, such as hand strikes.

The front and sidekicks are straight-line kicks and can generate a lot of power. Your round and hooking kicks are circular techniques and can be used effectively with your hands.

KICKING BALANCE

1) Make sure that you have upper body alignment with your kick.

2) Make sure that your hip is aligned with your target.

3) Make sure that your center of gravity is over your kick.

4) Pivot your back foot towards your target.

KICKING VARIATIONS

FRONT KICK
1. Front Leg
2. Back Leg
3. Snap
4. Thrust
5. Double
6. Jump
7. Step Infront
8. Skip In
9. Slide Up
10. Spin

SIDE KICK
1. Front Leg
2. Back Leg
3. Snap
4. Thrust
5. Double
6. Jump
7. Step Behind
8. Skip In
9. Slide Up
10. Spin

ROUND KICK
1. Front Leg
2. Back Leg
3. Thrust
4. Double
5. Jump
6. Slide Up
7. Step In Front
8. Jump In
9. Spin
10. Snap

HOOK KICK
1. Front Leg
2. Back Leg
3. Jump
4. Step Behind
5. Slide Up
6. Jump In
7. Spin
8. Step Out

FRONT KICK

The front kick, also referred to as the street fighter kick, is a straight-line kick that can be done effectively with both legs. This kick, like all of the other kicks, has many different variations. The striking surface of this kick can be the instep, ball of the foot, or bottom of the foot, and heel. Remember when throwing these kicks; pick your knee up to the height of the target.

To execute the front leg front kick, pick the knee up and as you thrust the foot out engage your hips by thrusting them forward. After you have thrown the kick, chamber it back and set it down.

ROUNDHOUSE KICKS

The roundhouse kick, also known as the round kick, is a very effective kick, which can be blended with other techniques smoothly. Round kicks can be thrown with either leg. The ball of the foot, shin, instep, and toes (with shoes on) are the striking surfaces for the round kick.

Targets can be any part of the body, with the main targets being the head, face, neck, stomach, groin, thigh, hip, floating rib, kidney, knee and calf.

To execute the front leg roundhouse kick, pick your knee up to the height of your target and point your knee about 3 to 4 inches past your target. Fire out the shin and foot; at the same time pivot your hips and back heel directly at the target for maximum power. The front leg round kick is used like a jab to set up other techniques. This kick can be performed while standing still, moving, or stepping, making it a versatile kicking technique.

SIDE KICK

The sidekick is a straight-line kick that is very powerful when thrown correctly. Sidekicks are mostly thrown with the front leg, except when performing the spinning back kick. The striking surface of the sidekick is the bottom of the foot, mainly the heel.

Targets for this powerful kick are the head, face, throat, chest, solar plexus, elbow, floating rib, stomach, groin, hips, thigh, knee, and shin.

To execute the front leg side kick bring your foot and knee up to the same level as your target and thrust your foot straight out. At the same time, pivot on your standing foot pointing the heel towards the target. When you make contact your foot and hips should be in a straight line.

HOOKING KICKS

The hooking kick is more of an advanced kick. It comes from the blind side making it a hard kick to see. The intent is to make contact with the heel. As with the other kicks, targets can be the whole body with the main targets being the face, head, neck, groin, and the thigh. I personally like to throw the hook kick to the lower line targets.

The hook kick travels in an arc, inside the line of attack to the point of impact and returns in the same manner as the round kick. By altering the height and direction of the kick, the foot may be brought down on an opponent, making it almost like an axe kick. When throwing your hook kick it's very important to get the knee as high as your target, and pivot the hips the same direction as your kick for maximum power.

SPIN KICKS

Spin kicks are great counter kicks; you can develop a lot of power with these types of kicks. Just about every kick can be done spinning, the most popular being the side and hook kicks, since they are the fastest and most powerful types of kicks. Again you should use spin kicks for low line targets in the street and, of course, higher line targets for sport.

When you throw these kicks it is very important that your head turns and picks up its target first. For illustration purposes, the spin backside kick is shown.

STEPPING KICKS

The Super "T" Karate student uses three different types of step kicks to close the distance. These types of kicks are mostly employed from the outside fighting range and usually follow your punches. Very seldom will you ever lead with this type of kick because it is so easy to see coming and your opponent will have a chance to get out of the way.

This section covers the different types of step kicks.

Remember that these kicks are used to close the distance between you and your opponent. The step will also increase the power in your kicks.

STEP BEHIND KICKS

Starting in your fighting stance, the step behind side kick is executed by taking a step around and behind your front foot, going past it about 12 inches while pointing the standing heel towards the target. Fire the kick out with your front foot. This type of step kick can also be done with a hop instead of the step to execute it much faster. For illustration purposes the sidekick is shown. The step behind movement can be done with the sidekick or hook kick.

SLIDE UP KICKS

Starting in your fighting stance, slide your back foot up to your front foot. As soon as the back foot hits the front foot, fire the front foot kick out. For illustration purposes the sidekick is shown. The slide up type of kicks can be done with the sidekick, hook kick, front kick, and roundhouse kick.

14 – Sparring

SPARRING

Through sparring you build confidence and overcome fear. Giving you the opportunity to put into action the techniques that you have learned. Sparring helps prepare you for self-defense by practicing your techniques under stress.

Sparring is a great way to improve timing, accuracy, balance, reflexes, stamina, awareness, offense, defense, footwork, and your grappling skills. Sparring helps you learn strategy.

While sparring you will quickly discover your strong and weak points, what works and what do not work under stress.

Sparring should never be an all out fight.

EIGHT REASON TO SPAR

1) Learn the ability to fight under stress.

2) Learn the ability to adapt to various situations.

3) Learn to protect yourself and fight when injured.

4) Learn how to withstand punishing strikes and be able to respond effectively.

5) Gain the ability to think and react under stress.

6) Learn to fight at any range with power and accuracy.

7) Develop footwork under pressure.

8) Learn control under stress.

FOUR DIFFERENT CONTACT LEVELS

In the Super "T" Karate System there are four different contact levels for sparring to ensure safety. Remember that control and safety is most important when sparring and that it is possible to get hurt no matter what level one is sparring at.

#1 - LIGHT CONTACT SPARRING

The first level is light contact sparring with absolutely no head contact. Light contact is allowed to the body with no strikes below the belt. The light contact level is used at the beginner level to help the student get use to and understand the concepts of sparring without the fear of being hurt.

#2 - MEDIUM CONTACT SPARRING

Medium contact sparring is the second level and is reserved for the intermediate and advanced student of the Super "T" Karate System.

At this level, harder contact is allowed to the groin, legs, head and body. This way the students can start to condition their body to contact.

Remember that control and safety is very important when sparring at this level, because the possibility of getting hurt is higher at this level. Make sure that you and your partner have a good understanding about the force of contact.

#3 - FULL CONTACT SPARRING

The third level is the full Contact level and is only for those students that have shown control and safety on the previous two sparring levels.

At this level the students spar with very hard contact to the legs, body, and head. The object at this level is to learn how to take and give punishment so one will be more prepared for the realities of the street.

Again control and safety is of the up most importance when sparring at this level. The possibility of being hurt is much higher. Remember that you are sparring to learn and not trying to knock each other out.

#4 - FREE STYLE

Free style sparring is the fourth level and utilizes all your techniques, including elbows, knees, kicks, punches, head butting and grappling. At this level of sparring the student can get familiarized with the reality of a real fight. But this level is not for everyone. Only after about one -and-a-half years of training in the basic techniques of stand up and ground work may a student, if they wish, be able to spar using free style techniques.

Students wishing to spar at the 2-4 levels must have approval from Master Terry and be supervised by an Instructor.

SPARRING EQUIPMENT

Sparring equipment is mandatory for all students that are doing any sparring dills or actual sparring. This equipment gives the student some added protection against injury and injuring their partner.

Equipment needed for light, medium and full contact sparring.

MANDATORY EQUIPMENT

Head Guard
Mouth Guard
14oz Boxing Gloves (adults)
8oz Karate Gloves (kids)
Groin Cup (male)
Shin or Shin and Instep Guards
Kickboots
Chest Guard

** Students that are sparring full contact must wear 16 oz gloves **

FREE STYLE SPARRING GEAR

Full Face Head Guard
Mouth Guard
Hand wraps
Chest and Body Guard
Groin Cup (male)
Shin or Shin and Instep Guards
Kickboots
Forearm Pads
Elbow and Knee Pads
Open Finger Gloves

DIFFERENT TYPES OF SPARRING

Their are many ways to work on fighting techniques. Each way has its own advantages. Here are a few different ways to spar.

Boxing vs. Boxing — Both students use only their hands to develop the upper body.

Boxing vs. Kicking — One student use only the hands, and the other student uses only the feet. This is a good way to discover what works and at what range it works.

Boxing vs. Kickboxing — One student again uses only hands, while the other uses the hands and feet. This will teach you what works and in what range it works at.

Kickboxing vs. Kickboxing — Both students are equal, using both hands and feet to do this type of sparring.

Freestyle vs. Kickboxing — Freestyle combines kickboxing with submission grappling.

SEVEN RULES OF FIGHTING

1) Never move back. If you must move back, do so moving in a side-to-side direction. Never move back in a straight line.

2) Never set yourself in one spot. Always move around, making it difficult for your opponent to plan an attack.

3) Always redirect your opponent. Never allow them to attack you head on.

4) Always fight your way. Don't get hooked into fighting their fight.

5) Place your opponent where you want them. Make them do just as you want them to do, so you may use counter strikes against them.

6) Remember that sparring is just that, and you are working on your moves and executing good control.

7) In a real fight do whatever it takes to survive the attack and come out the winner.

STRATEGY POINTERS

1) A successful fighter is a thinking fighter who can outmaneuver a slugger, boxer, and a grappler, picking them off at will. Fight with your brains not your brawn.

2) Use a variety of techniques. If your opponent protects his head well, avoid the head and go down to the body and vise versa.

3) When caught against the wall or in a corner escape by slipping to the sides and around your opponent.

4) Do not rush in wildly at your opponent. Attack only when there is an opening and the possibility of hitting your target.

5) Apply faking techniques throughout your fighting to assess your opponent's reaction.

6) When sparring, work with an assortment of different fighters, tall, short, fast, slow, kickers, punchers, grapplers, aggressive, defensive, etc. Each fighter will offer you a variety of challenges calling on you to add and subtract tactics from your fight strategy.

7) Keep your fight game basic, do not try techniques that look good but cannot get the job done. If a technique does not work, discard it.

FIGHTING RANGES

The Super "T" Karate System utilizes three fighting ranges to cover the distances in fighting. It is very important that you know and understand what techniques can be executed from each of the three ranges effectively. You also need to learn how to get from one range to the other safely and effectively.

#1 - **Outside Range**: This range is also known as the safe zone. Step, slide up, and long kicks can all be thrown effectively at this range.

#2 - **Mid Range**: This is probably the most popular range as your kicks and long punches work very well at this distance.

#3 - **Inclose or Inside Range**: This is the range that you should really avoid when fighting a skilled fighter, if at all possible. At this range your knees, elbows and short punches (like the uppercuts and hooks) become the main weapons. Biting, hair pulling, holding and hitting, head butting, and grappling all come into play in this range, so there is a lot more to look out for. That is why it is best to avoid this range if at all possible.

OFFENSE

There is a saying in sports that in order to win you need to have a good defense. In fighting there is no way to win without a good offense because you cannot win a fight on defense alone. To win a fight you must either knock out your opponent or put them in a submission hold to stop them from attacking you.

FEINTING

To feint you must make it look like you are going to attack your opponent on one side or a part of the body, so when they react to the feint, you can attack another part that is not covered up.

To do an effective feint you can use your feet, hands, body or eyes in an effort to deceive your opponent. Make the movement real so your opponent will think that you are going to use it. Before they can adjust, you take advantage of the opening that you just have created.

Feinting will also help you to find out how your opponent will react to a certain technique. In order to become good at feinting and make it believable, one must practice them often. Remember to react instantly when an opening occurs. Don't feint often or your opponent will start to get use to it and counter when you do the feints.

BLITZING

1) The reason behind this is obvious. The less time spent getting from the out of range position to your opponent, the less time they have to hit you as you come in.

2) You want to hit your opponent with a barrage of shots to different areas of the body so they cannot possibly block every shot. Also the feeling of getting hit rapidly and in different areas of the body tends to overwhelm and offset your opponent.

3) Unexpected and sudden movements can cause time lags and hesitancy in your opponent's reactions which can give you an advantage.

4) The more thrust there is off of your rear leg in your charge, the more physical mass speed you will have.

FAKING

When throwing a fake, you have to establish whether your opponent reacts to a body movement or technique. Most people will respond to a body fake.

HIGH / LOW: Has to do with up and down faking. You fake high and then attack low or just the opposite, fake low and then attack high.

SIDE / SIDE: Move to the right and attack to the left, or go to the left and attack to the right.

BODY FAKING: Use a sharp motion of the hips and/or shoulders to appear as if you are attacking so you will get a reaction out of them.

ATTACK BY DRAWING

BAIT / This is done simply by leaving an area open. When your opponent attacks, cover the area or shift its position out of the line of attack. Look for the hole that they leave open as they attack and go for it.

PULL / This is good for driving your opponent crazy. Basically you keep stepping just out of range of attack or stay totally away from them until there patience breaks and they come after you full bore. Then you either run or pick them off with counter shots, depending on what options you have at the time.

ATTACK BY TRAPPING

GRABBING / This is usually done during your entry into your opponent's range. When you grab, pull your opponent towards you, taking him off balance and into your strike.

15 – Pain Points

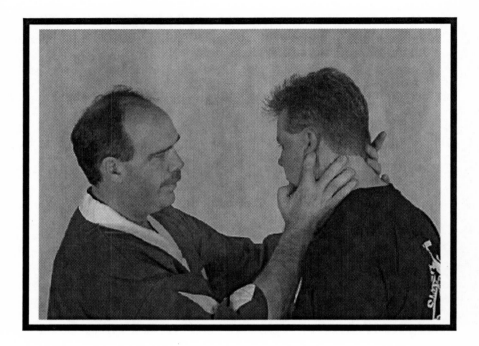

PAIN POINTS

Pain points are sensitive places on the body also referred to as pressure points. In this section we will cover some of the most effective pain points found in the head and face area.

These pain points have a different effect on different size people. With this in mind, it's very important to practice these points with both male and female partners.

WARNING: Pain points can cause severe pain, practice them with caution.

The pain points shown in this section have proven highly effective by Terry throughout his 25 plus years of martial arts training. Pain points are done to loosen up an opponent and distract them to get them off guard so you can apply a follow up technique.

When performing a pain point on someone it's important to hold the area still and solid. When you apply a pain point technique, push and hold the point very firmly with one or two fingers. When striking a pain point the strike needs to be a solid and stiff blow to be effective.

HYPOGLOSSAL NERVE

Nerve that it effects: Hypoglossal.
Location: Approximately one inch from the back of the jaw and one inch deep.
Application: Pushing pressure penetration with the thumb or two fingers.
Effects: Submission, stunning.

MANDIBULAR ANGLE

Nerve that it effects: Hypoglossal.
Location: Under the ear lobe.
Application: Pushing pressure penetration with the thumb or fingers.
Effects: Submission

INFRA ORBITAL

Nerve that it effects: Infra orbital.
Location: Base of nose.
Application: Pushing pressure motion on a 45-degree angle towards the crown of the head.
Effects: Watering of the eyes, stunning.

JUGULAR NOTCH

Nerve that it effects: Superior Laryngeal
Location: Jugular notch region.
Application: Quick thrusting with two fingers.
Effects: Stunning, Distraction

SUPRASCAPULAR NERVE MOTOR

Nerve that it effects: Suprascapular
Location: Side of the neck where the trapezius muscle connects to the side of the neck.
Application: Hammer fist strike going on an angle towards the ground.
Effects: Temporary motor dysfunction that may effect the arm or hand on the same side that is hit.

BRACHIAL PLEXES ORIGIN

Nerve that it effects: Radial.
Location: Side of the neck in the middle.
Application: Pressure by pushing thumb or fingers. Strikes using the hammer fist, palm heel, or a punch.
Effects: By pressure submission. By strikes possible unconsciousness or distraction.

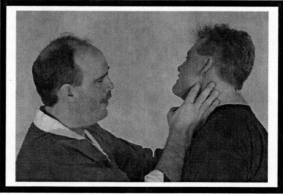

16 – Grappling

GRAPPLING

As a stand up fighter you don't want to be on the ground grappling with anyone. So you first need to do what you can to avoid going to the ground or into a grappling situation with your footwork, kicks, punches, elbow and knee strikes. One thing that you really should understand about fighting is that you don't box with a boxer and you don't kick with a kicker. So then, why grapple with a grappler? You should kick with a boxer, box with a kicker, and box and kick with a grappler. Your footwork and balance is very important when facing a grappler.

When a grappler is grabbing you they are tying up their hands, so you should be using all of the strikes that you have in your arsenal.

Also remember that if you do end up on the ground you have your teeth, elbows, knees, and head for head butts. These are all very good for close in fighting.

On the ground or in a grappling positions keep in close to your opponent to make it very hard for them to mount an offense. Suck on to them like a leech and don't let go. Keeping your body weight to the side of them with your feet spread apart makes it very hard for them to roll you or pick you up to slam you.

Recognizing that it is possible for a stand up fighter to be taken down to the ground, the next five sections are dedicated to covering some basic skills used in grappling so you will be familiar with what a grappler may try and do.

GRAPPLING

The grappling can be done either from the left side or the right side. Remember when you practice to be very careful as these moves can cause severe injury.

When a throw is executed correctly there will be a pause when the takedown knocks the wind out of them. This will allow you to react and apply a finishing hold to them.

Remember that in a fight you need to do whatever it takes to come out the victor. If that means eye poking, ear twisting, fish hooking, sticking your fingers in your opponent's nostril, hair pulling, biting, grabbing, twisting, and breaking of the thumb and fingers, then do it.

GROUND CONTROL POSITIONS

Having a dominant controlling position on the ground when ground fighting is essential to be able to deliver effective strikes and submission holds.

This section will cover three highly effective ground-controlling positions of the Super "T" Karate System.

Beware because in a street fight anything goes including eye poking, biting, fish hooking, ear twisting, hair pulling, head butting and anything else that it takes to survive an attack. Don't just rely on these basic positions, even though they will help you mount a better offense. Remember to do whatever it takes to survive an attack and try to stay up on your feet.

FULL MOUNT POSITION

The full mount position is a very devastating and controlling position for strikes and is a difficult position from which to escape. When your opponent tries to escape it opens up great submission opportunities for you.

The full mount is so devastating that most fights are over once someone obtains this position. **This is one position that you want to avoid being on the bottom of at all cost.** There are several keys to help maintain the top position so you can have the upper hand in a fight.

First, keep your weight forward so they can't buck you off. Do this by putting your knees up and under your opponent's armpits. This also helps protect your groin because they won't have any leverage to get any real power into their strikes. At the same time you should be raining down strikes on them making it almost impossible for them to mount an offense.

The second way to keep the full mount is to grapevine their legs and lay all your body weight on them while applying a submission hold.

If you find yourself on the bottom of the full mount, pull your opponent's head down close to yours. At the same time you should

97

be biting, eye poking, pulling hair, or whatever you can to get them off of you.

GUARD POSITIONS

The guard position is the position you should try to attain if you are on your back. This position can help to prevent your opponent from getting the full mount position.

The guard also puts you and your opponent at the same level so you will be able to strike him too. From this position you can mount an offense with strikes and submissions, eye poking, ear twisting, fish hooking, head butting, and other types of brutal techniques.

SIDE CONTROL POSITION

Any smart fighter will not let you get the full mount position, so the next best thing is the side control position. From this position you can neutralize your opponent's offense and attack him with your elbows, knee strikes, and effective submission holds.

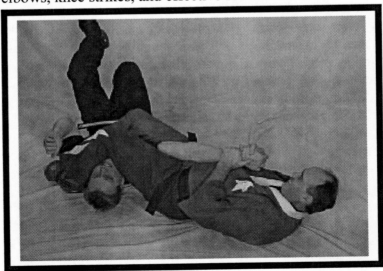

17 – Takedowns

TAKEDOWNS

Takedowns are used to get your opponent down to the ground so you may control him or escape. When a takedown is performed correctly it can be very punishing.

This section will cover different types of takedowns, throws and foot sweeps found within the Super "T" Karate System.

The takedowns and throws demonstrated here probably won't go down in a fight as smoothly as they are demonstrated here, but the mechanics and moves work in a lot of different situations. Practice the takedowns and throws often so the mechanics become second nature to you.

HIP THROW

Right sided hip throw: Grab your opponent's right arm with your left hand; step through with your right foot putting your right hip against his. Then place your right hand on his hip and squat down a little. Pick him up as you straighten out your legs, twisting him over your hip. If he is too heavy, you can roll him over your leg. To do a left sided hip throw the opposite will apply.

KNEE THROW

The technique utilized to execute the knee throw is similar to the hip throw. Right sided knee throw: Grab your opponent's right hand with your left, place your right knee behind his right knee and put your right hand on his shoulder (or you can put it around the neck). Push with your right hand and pull with your left at the same time. Sweeping his leg from beneath him.

WINDING THROW

When your opponent grabs you with one or two hands you can apply a winding throw by taking one hand and bringing it over the top of their arm (or arms) and hit them with an elbow to the face. At the same time, twist your body into his arms tightly, winding like a top. Drop down to one knee while twisting and he will go over your shoulder.

SHOULDER THROW

When your opponent throws a punch step into it, catching it at the elbow. Put your shoulder tight against his body holding the arm tight and close to you. Drop to one knee and twist, pushing your shoulder towards the ground so your opponent will go over top of you.

18 – Chokes

CHOKES

There are two types of chokes in the Super "T" System. The first one is the respiratory choke, which applies pressure on the trachea (wind pipe). **WARNING: This is a very deadly choke.**

The second choke and probably the most popular, is called the sleeper choke. To do this you put pressure on the side of the neck establishing control of the blood supply to the brain. By shutting off the blood supply to the brain temporarily you can render an opponent unconscious within 5-8 seconds if the technique is applied correctly. **WARNING: You should never practice this technique to the point of unconsciousness.**

WARNING: Chokes are extremely dangerous and should only be practiced with extreme caution and under qualified supervision.

Here is a tip when applying chokes out on the street for self defense. After you apply the choke count to eight and, while maintaining your position, loosen up on the choke to see if they are finished fighting you. If your opponent starts to fight again, tighten back up on the technique. If they are not resisting, release the choke and get away or get help if they are unconscious.

SPECIAL NOTE:

If your opponent is rendered unconscious they should regain consciousness within 5-30 seconds. You can attempt to revive them by raising them to a seated position and delivering a sharp slap between the shoulder blades.

If you fail to revive them within 30 seconds, loosen the clothing around their neck, start CPR and Call for HELP right away.

RESPIRATORY CHOKE

You should never apply a respiratory type of choke (wind pipe) unless your life is in danger and there is absolutely no other choice but to apply that type of choke. You will definitely know when you are applying a respiratory type of choke because your opponent will most definitely fight to get out.

SLEEPER CHOKE

Sleeper chokes are used to control your opponent. When applied correctly they will become relaxed and stop fighting with you. Remember, if they are struggling with you it means that you don't have the technique applied correctly. You should make an adjustment to apply the technique correctly.

19 – Self-Defense

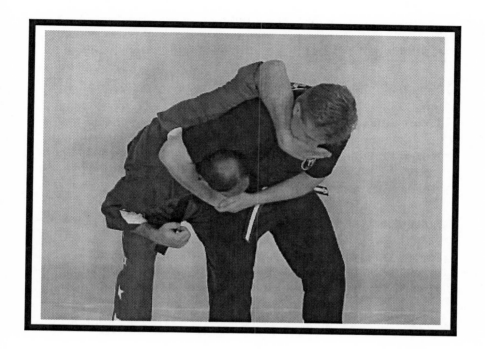

REAL SELF DEFENSE

Some techniques are for sport, showmanship or TV, and have no real value in true self-defense. Real self-defense techniques bear no resemblance to what you see in a movie or even in most martial arts schools.

To be effective in real self-defense all of your techniques should be simple, direct and to the point to stop an attack. Never rely on or expect to do the job with just one technique. Be prepared and ready to use follow up techniques so you can get away. Here is a list that I put together of some of the things that you should and should not do in a real self-defense situation.

Remember that in a real self-defense situation anything goes and you must do whatever it takes to survive the attack. If that means to bite, pull hair, fish hook the mouth; poke the eyes, etc., so be it.

THINGS NOT TO DO

1) Never get into your opponent's face.

2) Never ever turn your back on your opponent.

3) Never put your hand up in a fighting stance with closed fists.

4) Never push your opponent.

5) Never stand with the front of your body facing your opponent.

6) Never use insulting words, as you are trying not to fight.

THINGS TO DO

1) Stand side ways at an angle to move your vital area out of the line of attack.

2) Make sure that you are at a safe distance so they have to move in to attack.

3) Learn to read body language.

4) Put your hands up in an open defense position.

5) Use your mouth to try and talk your way out of fighting.

6) Talk with your hands, keep your hands moving so you will be able to react faster if they attack you.

7) If you know that a fight is going to happen, hit first.

8) Fake high and strike low.

ENVIRONMENTAL DEFENSE

The way that society is today we must be prepared for an attack any time and any place. It could happen in your home, office, car, or when you just go outside for a walk.

This section covers some ideas that may prepare you for that scary moment that may or may not happen. Section 21 covered self defense techniques using the body. This section will cover weapons in the environment that may be at your disposal to help you over come and escape an attack.

You need to be aware of your surroundings and what can be used as weapons if you are attacked. It is very important for personal protection to familiarize yourself with what can be used in any given place as a weapon. When under a combat situation your mind could go blank so you can't think straight. That is why I think it is so important to go over this and practice in different places such as your living room, hallway, yard, etc.

MALE

COINS: Coins can be used to throw into the face of an attacker to distract them.

KEYS: Your keys are great weapons to poke the eyes or scratch the face and neck. You can even put them into your hands between your fingers and strike with them.

COMB: A comb can be a very brutal weapon as you rake it across the eyes and face.

BELT: Your belt can used to strike with and as a choking weapon.

WOMEN

COINS: Coins can be used to throw into the face of an attacker to distract them.

KEYS: Your keys are great weapons to poke the eyes or scratch the face and neck. You can even put them into your hands between your fingers and strike with them.

BRUSH: A brush can be used as a club as well as something to scratch the face and eyes.

PERFUME & HAIR SPRAY: Perfume and hair spray can be sprayed into the attacker's eyes.

LIPSTICK, MASCARA, AND EYE SHADOW PENCIL: All of these items can be used to poke the eyes. Placed into your hand so that it protrudes out of the bottom of your fist, you can strike with a hammer fist.

PURSE: A purse can be used like a club.

OFFICE

PHONE: The phone can be used for clubbing or calling 911.
PEN & PENCILS: Pen and Pencil can be used for poking the eyes or stabbing the body.
CHAIR: A chair can be used to keep the attacker away from you or to club them.
STAPLER: A stapler can be used as a club or even to staple them.
BOOKS: Books can be used for striking and clubbing.
THREE HOLE PUNCH: The big binder punch can be used for clubbing.

HOME

SILVERWARE: Forks and knifes can be used to slash or stab an attacker.
BROOM: Broom handle can be used to poke and as a club.
PHONE: The phone can be used to club with and for call 911.
LAMP: Lamps and other figurines can be used as a club.
CHAIR: A chair can be used to keep the attacker away from you or to club them.
PLANT SOIL, COFFEE, SUGAR, Etc.: Throw into the eyes to distract and blind your attacker.
DISHES: Use as a club.

CAR

LIGHTER: Used for striking and to burn your attacker.
PEN & PENCILS: Pen and Pencils can be used for poking the eyes or stabbing the body.
CELL PHONE: Call 911 and can be used as a club.
KEYS: Your keys are great weapons to poke the eyes or scratch the face and neck. You can even put them into your hands between your fingers and punch with them.

KEY POINTS FOR SELF DEFENSE

1) Recognize potentially dangerous situations, never let your guard down.

2) Avoid dangerous situations. Avoidance is the best method of self-defense.

3) Use any method it takes to escape (at all cost), as it might be a matter of life or death.

4) Try to make the attackers relaxed and off guard so you may attack when they least expect it.

5) Defend yourself as the last resort and don't hesitate to commit yourself totally, decisively, powerfully, and quickly.

6) Remember that most of the vital target areas are in the center part of your body (referred to as the centerline).

7) Get your body out of the line of attack.

8) If you are grabbed, use some distraction techniques like a foot stomp, head butt, groin grab, etc. to help set up other techniques or to help you escape.

TARGET AREAS

- **CHIN**
- **TEMPLE**
- **NECK**
- **EYES**
- **EARS**
- **THROAT**
- **GROIN**
- **NOSE**
- **SHINS**
- **KNEES**

20 – Elbow and Knee Strikes

ELBOW STRIKES

Elbow strikes are some of the most brutal and dangerous techniques you will find in the Super "T" Karate System. Elbows are thrown from the inclose range just like knee strikes, using your body weight, and can be thrown with both arms. The striking surface is the point of the elbow making it a very painful and devastating strike. The most damaging targets for elbows strikes are from the neck up. Elbow strikes can also be used effectively on the ground while in a grappling situation.

Your elbows are the most effective when thrown at shoulder level.

Elbow strikes are performed using the same principles as your punches and can be done with the front or backhand. Elbow strikes work the best when they follow a technique such as a jab punch or a power punch.

UP ELBOW

When throwing the up elbow, keep your arm and elbow in close and tight to your body. At the same time you thrust your elbow up, twist your back foot the same direction. Targets for the up elbow are the chest, chin, nose, and the eye socket.

DOWN ELBOW

To throw the down elbow pick your elbow up above your target and drive it straight down. Put your body weight into it while doing this. Targets for the down elbow are the neck, collarbone, spine, and kidney.

ACROSS ELBOW

When you execute the across elbow it will look almost like a hook punch and the principals are the same. Targets are the jaw, temple, nose, cheek, and neck.

PULL BACK ELBOW

You do this elbow almost like doing a backhand strike. The targets are the jaw, cheek, temple, nose, neck, and back of the head.

3/4 UP ELBOW

The 3/4 up elbow comes in at a very devastating angle. When throwing this powerful elbow strike you will bring it up on a 3/4 angle across your body. The targets are the chin, nose, eye socket, and cheek.

3/4 DOWN ELBOW

Just like the 3/4 up elbow strike the 3/4 down elbow comes from a very difficult angle to detect and has a lot of power. Targets for this technique are the cheek, nose, neck, and collarbone.

SPIN ELBOW

This elbow strike is just like a spinning back fist, except you do not snap the hand out, you keep it in and strike with the elbow. Targets for this strike are the head and neck areas.

KNEE STRIKES

Knee strikes are a very brutal and devastating technique that must be performed in the inclose range, just like your elbow strikes, to be effective. You will find three different types of knee strikes in the Super "T" Karate System.

UP KNEE

The striking surface of this knee strike is the top of the knee. It is a very simple knee strike to throw, targeting the groin, chest, and face. While performing this knee strike you can increase its impact and power by grabbing around the neck or shoulders of your opponent and pulling them into the knee.

Throwing the up knee strike: As you bring the knee straight up, pull the heel of the striking leg towards you, keeping your knee bent tightly. At the same time, thrust your hip forward and pull both your head and shoulders back.

3/4 KNEE

The 3/4 knee is also referred to as the roundhouse knee, with the striking surface being the same as the up knee. Targets for this explosive knee strike are the groin, leg, stomach, and the side of the leg. Executing the 3/4 knee is much like throwing a 3/4 leg kick but the foot does not go out. Just like throwing the up knee, bring your heel back towards you and keep your leg bent as tightly as possible.

THAI KNEE

The up & over knee strike, also referred to as the Thai knee, is the third knee strike of the Super "T" Karate System. This knee strike is a little more advanced, with the striking surface being the inner side of the knee. Targets for this knee are the side of the head, face, body, and floating rib. To execute the Thai knee strike, raise the knee straight up while pulling the heel back and keeping the leg bent tightly. Now twist your hips while thrusting the knee towards your target.

666

666666666

66666

21 – Belt Rank Requirements

Belt Ranking Time Requirements

Jr. and Adult Ranks	# Of Classes	Minimum Months
White Belt to Orange Belt	16	2
Orange Belt to Orange / Stripe	20	2
Orange / Stripe to Yellow Belt	20	2
Yellow Belt to Yellow / Stripe	20	2
Yellow / Stripe to Green Belt	20	2
Green Belt to Green / Stripe	20	2
Green / Stripe to Purple Belt	20	2
Purple Belt to Purple / Stripe	20	2
Purple / Stripe to Brown Belt	24	3
Brown Belt to Brown / Stripe	24	3
Brown / Stripe to Candidate Black Belt	30	3
Candidate Black Belt to 1st Degree Black Belt	72	12
1st Degree Black Belt to 2nd Degree Black Belt	124	18
2nd Degree Black Belt to 3rd Degree Black Belt	160	24

3rd Degree and above will be awarded based on age and "time served": With the minimum of 2 - 5 years between Degrees and service to the S.T.K.A.

116

Under Black Belt Ranks

Solid Orange Belt -- Beginner Rank

Orange Stripe Belt -- Beginner Rank

Solid Yellow Belt -- Beginner Rank

Yellow Stripe Belt – Intermediate Rank

Solid Green Belt – Intermediate Rank

Green Stripe Belt – Intermediate Rank

Purple Belt – Intermediate Rank

Purple Stripe Belt -- Advance Rank

Solid Brown Belt -- Advance Rank

Brown Stripe Belt -- Advance Rank

Color Belt Ranking Require ments

Progress Checks, Striping, and Testing.

Super T Karate students go through a progress / striping for the first two color stripes every eight classes. The red stripe is the pre-test and will be preformed after twenty classes to see if they are ready to test for their next belt rank. Students that did not earn their stripe will be allowed to try again after a couple of classes.

At the Exam / Graduation they will perform the second stage of their test as with the Blue and Red stripes they must perform with speed, power, intensity to graduate to the next rank, if for some reason they do not earn their next belt rank they will be able to try again on the next testing month.

Testing Application

All students that have earned their Red stripe must submit an testing application for their next belt rank this application must be filled out completely and neatly so it my be process.

ORANGE BELT:
- Kicking Set #1
- Kickboxing Sets 1 – 3
- Footwork Set 1&2
- Flexibility

ORANGE / STRIPE BELT:

- Blocking Sets 1-6
- Kicking Set #1
- Kickboxing Sets 1 – 3
- One Hand Grab Defense
- Flexibility

YELLOW BELT:

- Kickboxing Sets 1-5
- Boxing Sets 1&2
- Kicking Sets 1&2
- Footwork Sets 1-4
- Flexibility

YELLOW / STRIPE BELT:

- Blocking Sets 1-6
- Kickboxing Sets 1-5
- Boxing Sets 1&2
- Kicking Sets 1-3
- Two Hand Grab Defense
- Flexibility

GREEN BELT:

- Kicking Sets 1-5
- Defense Sets 1-4
- Kickboxing Sets 1-6
- Step Kicks
- Boxing Sets 1-4
- Flexibility

GREEN / STRIPE BELT:

- Kicking Sets 1-5
- Step Kicks
- Defense Sets 1-4
- Kickboxing Sets 1-6
- Boxing Sets 1-4
- Side Head Lock Defense
- Flexibility

PURPLE BELT:

- Boxing Sets 1-5
- Kicking Sets 1-5
- Kickboxing Sets 1-7
- Defensive Sets 1-4
- Elbow Sets 1-6
- Self Defense
- Flexibility

PURPLE / STRIPE BELT:

- Boxing Sets 1-6
- Elbow Sets 1-6
- Kicking Sets 1-5
- Combination KATA
- Kickboxing Sets 1-7
- Defensive Sets 1-4
- Step Kicks
- Flexibility

BROWN BELT:

- Kickboxing Sets 1-7
- Blocking Sets 1-6
- Boxing Sets 1-6
- Kicking Sets 1-5
- Defensive Sets 1-4
- Self Defense
- Push Ups & Sit Ups
- Flexibility

BROWN / STRIPE BELT:

- Kickboxing Sets 1-7
- Blocking Sets 1-6
- Boxing Sets 1-6
- Kicking Sets 1-5
- Defensive Sets 1-4
- Self Defense
- Push Ups & Sit Ups
- All Kicks
- Flexibility

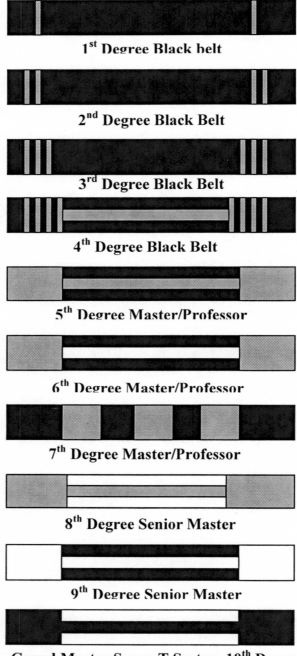

1st Degree Black belt

2nd Degree Black Belt

3rd Degree Black Belt

4th Degree Black Belt

5th Degree Master/Professor

6th Degree Master/Professor

7th Degree Master/Professor

8th Degree Senior Master

9th Degree Senior Master

Grand Master Super T System 10th Degree

Jr. / Candidate Black Belt

1 – Age Requirements
Minimum age of 8 years old is required to hold this rank.

2 - Requirements
a. Minimum of 220 classes and 24 months
b. Testing Sections

Section 1 -- Techniques
Kickboxing Sets 1-7, Defensive Sets 1-4, Boxing Sets1-6,
Blocking Sets 1-6,
& Kicking Kata

Section 2 -- Self Defense
One Hand Grabs, Two Hand Grabs, Head Lock Defense,
Mount Defense & Choke Defense

Section 3 -- Strength & Flexibility

GROUP	PUSH UPS	SIT UPS
8 Years of Age	10	25
9 Yrs. and 10 Yrs.	15	35
11 Yrs. To 13 Yrs.	20	40
14 Yrs. To 16 Yrs.	25	50
Adult Men	35	60
Adult Women	25	50

FLEXIBILITY
Kids under 14 years of age Side or Front Splits
Adults - Standing floor touch with palms -- Inleg and Straddle Stretch head to knee

Section 4 -- Pad Work

Focus Mitts – 1rd Jabs, 1rd Two-Punch Combo, 1rd Round Kicks, 1rd Hands & Feet.

Kick Shield – 1rd Front Kicks, 1rd Side Kicks, 1rd Round Kicks, 1rd Mix Kicks

Section 5 – Sparring
2rd Boxing, 2rds Kickboxing

1 – Age Requirements
Minimum age of 9 years old is required to hold this rank.

2 - Requirements
a. Attended a minimum of 10 Black Belt Classes since last testing.
b. 72 training classes including Black Belt Classes and 12 months since last Test.
c. Letter of recommendation from a teacher or a friend of the family.
d. Testing Sections

Section 1 -- Techniques
Kickboxing Sets 1-7, Defensive Sets 1-4, Boxing Sets 1-6, Blocking Sets 1-6

Section 2 -- Self Defense
One Hand Grabs, Two Hand Grabs, Head Lock Defense, Mount Defense & Choke Defense

Section 3 -- Strength & Flexibility
See Requirements on Jr. / candidate Testing

Section 4 -- Pad Work
Focus Mitts – 2rds. Hands, 2rds Feet, 1rd Hands & Feet

Kick Shield – 2rds Straight-line Kicks, 2rds Round Kicks, 1rd Mix Kicks

Section 5 -- Sparring
2rd Boxing, 2rds Kickboxing

Section 6 – Kata
Naihanchi Kata, & Kicking Kata

3 – Partners
All testing students are responsible to provide their own sparring and self-defense partners.

4. Appearance
1. Kick Pants, Belt and T-shirt for Pre-Testing and Test
2. Full Uniform for Belt Ceremony.

DEFENSIVE SETS

Blocking Sets
#1 – Left Hand Low
#2 – Right Hand Low
#3 – Left Hand In
#4 – Right Hand In
#5 – Left Hand V-Block
#6 – Right Hand V-Block

Defensive Sets
#1 – Left Slip
#2 – Right Slip
#3 – Left Bob
#4 – Right Bob

Footwork Sets
#1 – Forward Shuffle
#2 – Back Shuffle
#3 – Right Shuffle
#4 – Left Shuffle

WEAPON SETS 1

Nuchucku Short Form 1
1 - Bow / drop one chuck down
2 - Reverse spin / Over right shoulder catch
3 - Slide Left foot out into Horse stance
4 - Right hand figure eight spin
5 - Leg cradle
6 - Over right shoulder catch
7 - Cross body behind back catch
8 - Over left shoulder catch
9 - Left hand figure eight spin
10 - Leg cradle
11 - Over left shoulder catch
12 - Cross body behind back catch
13 - Over right shoulder catch / Slide Left leg out into Guard stance
14 - Raise chucks above head / Step forward with right leg & spin while swinging chucks
15 - Tap left leg / Tap right leg / Over right shoulder catch
16 - Slide Left foot back / Put chucks together / Bow

KAMA Set #1
1 – Power Horse Stance
2 - Left Side Chop/ Right Hand Down Chop
3 – Right Side Chop / Left Hand Down Chop
4 – Down the Middle Horse Stance / Two Hand Down Chop / Spin KAMA's
5 –Spin Around Left Hand / Side Chop
6 – Jump Front Kick
7 – Power Bow Stance

Broad Sword
1 - Concentration Stance
2 - Stab Front Stance
3 - Spin Around Stab
4 - Right Side Back Stab and Swipe
5 - Figure Eight
6 - Back Leg Front Kick to Concentration Stance looking to Left
7 - Stab Front Stance
8 - Stab to Left
9 - Right Side Back Stab and Swipe
10 - Crane Stance to Back

STRIKING

SETS

Kickboxing Sets
#1- Double Jab / Power
#2- Left Bob & Weave / Hook / Power
#3- Right Knee / Left Knee
#4- Right Elbow / Left Elbow
#5- Right Round Kick / Left Round Kick
#6- Power / Hook / Step Infront Round Kick
#7- Jab / Power / Back Elbow

BOXING SETS
#1 – Jab – Hook (same hand) / Power
#2 – Jab / Power / Hook
#3 – Power / Hook / Power
#4 – Front Hand Uppercut / Power / Hook
#5 – B/H Uppercut / F/H Uppercut / Power / Hook
#6 – Power / Body & Head Hook / Power / Hook

Kick Sets
#1 - Back Leg Front / Round Kick
#2 - Front Leg Round / Back Leg Front / Round Kick
#3 - Side Kick / Step Behind Side Kick / Back Leg Round Kick
#4 - Front Leg Round Kick / Step Behind Side Kick / Back Leg Front Kick
#5 - Back Leg Round Kick / Spin Back Hook Kick

Elbow Sets

#1 - Back Across / Front Across
#2 - Back Up / Front Up
#3 - Back 3/4 Down / Front 3/4 Down

SUPER T

KATA

BLACK BELT CHAMPIONS
Since 1979

COMBINATION KATA
1 – Bow Fighting Stance (ki)
2 - Jab / Side Kick
3 – Jab / Power / Back Leg Round Kick
4 – Spin Back Kick
5 – Front Hand Uppercut / Power / Hook
6 – Step Infront Round Kick
7 – Back Leg Front Kick
8 – Return Back to Stance

KICKING KATA
1- Bow Fighting Stance (KI)
2- Right Leg Front Kick
3- Left Leg Front Kick
4- Step in Front Round Kick
5- Step Behind Side Kick
6- Back Leg Round Kick
7- Spin Back Kick
8- Back Leg Outward Crescent Kick
9- Left Leg Round Kick
10- Return Back to Stance Bow

WEAPON

SET 2

Nunchucku Set #1
1 – Right hand forward spin
2 – Right hand figure eight spin
3 – Between legs right back two hand under arm catch
4 – Left hand back under arm catch
5 – Left hand forward spin
6 – Left hand figure eight spin
7 – Between legs left back two hand under arm catch
8 – Right two hand under arm catch

Nunchucku Set #2
1 – Right hand forward spin
2 – Right hand figure eight spin
3 – Between legs Right hand back under arm catch
4 – Left hand reverse under arm catch
5 – Right hand reverse under arm catch
6 – Right hand across back catch
7 – Butt bounce Left hand across the back catch
8 – Right hand two hand under arm catch

Bo-Staff #1
1 – Right over the shoulder flip
2 – Down strike on Left side
3 – Side to side
4 – Spear
5 – Right hand figure eight spin
6 –Power Stance

Bo-Staff # 2

1 – Right Hand Spin / Two Hand Spin / Left Hand Spin / Two Hand Spin

2 – Step Forward with the Right Foot Down Strike / Straight Stab (KI)

3 – Spin Around with the Left Foot Side Strike / Spin Back Around with Left Foot Side Strike.

4 – Behind the Back Grab / Sip Around the Body

5 – Two Hand Above the Head Spin Grab / Behind the Back Grab

6 – Step Forward with the Left Foot Toe Strike (KI)

7 – Slide Left Foot Back to Right Foot / Two Hand Spin

8 – Feet Together Bo Staff angled on the Ground

9 – Slide Left Foot Out Shoulder width / Left Knife Hand (KI)

SUPER T
TECHNIQUES

Kicks

- Front
- Side
- Round
- Back
- Hook
- In & Out Crescent
- Cross
- Angle
- Step Behind Side
- Step Infront Round
- Step Behind Hook
- Step Behind Crescent
- Step Infront Front
- Spin Back
- Spin Hook
- Spin Crescent Jump Kicks
- Slide Up Kicks

Blocking

- Inward
- Outward
- High
- Low
- V-Block
- Check

Hand Strikes

- Back Fist
- Ridge Hand
- Palm
- Jab
- Power
- Hook
- Uppercut
- Vertical Punch

Printed in the United States
200059BV00008B/319-378/A

9 781598 242102